Step-by-Step Transformations

Turning Oranges into Juice

Jerome Hawkins

Cavendish
Square

New York

Published in 2015 by Cavendish Square Publishing, LLC
243 5th Avenue, Suite 136, New York, NY 10016

First Edition

Website: cavendishsq.com

This publication represents the opinions and views of the author based on his or her personal experience, knowledge, and research. The information in this book serves as a general guide only. The author and publisher have used their best efforts in preparing this book and disclaim liability rising directly or indirectly from the use and application of this book.

CPSIA Compliance Information: Batch #WS14CSQ

All websites were available and accurate when this book was sent to press.

Hawkins, Jerome.
Turning oranges into juice / Jerome Hawkins.
pages cm. — (Step-by-step transformations)
Includes bibliographical references and index.
ISBN 978-1-62713-016-5 (hardcover) ISBN 978-1-62713-017-2 (paperback) ISBN 978-1-62713-018-9 (ebook)
1. Orange juice—Juvenile literature. 2. Oranges—Juvenile literature. I. Title. II. Series: Step-by-step transformations.

TP441.C5H38 2014
664'.80431—dc23

2014002061

Editorial Director: Dean Miller
Editor: Amy Hayes
Copy Editor: Cynthia Roby
Art Director: Jeffrey Talbot
Designer: Joseph Macri
Photo Researcher: J8 Media
Production Manager: Jennifer Ryder-Talbot
Production Editor: David McNamara

The photographs in this book are used by permission and through the courtesy of: Cover photos by Martin Poole/The Image Bank/Getty Images; Nitr/Shutterstock.com; © iStockphoto.com/Floortje, 5; David Sutherland/Photographer's Choice/Getty Images, 7; © David R. Frazier Photolibrary, Inc./Alamy, 9; © David R. Frazier Photolibrary, Inc./Alamy, 11; Luis Davilla/The Image Bank/Getty Images, 13; Luis Davilla/Cover/Getty Images, 15; ©Jim West/The Image Works, 17; Andy Sotiriou/Photodisc/Gety Images, 19; Exactostock/SuperStock, 21; Back cover by Dave and Les Jacobs/Blend Images/Getty Images.

Printed in the United States of America

Contents

Orange juice is made
from oranges.

4

Oranges grow on trees.

The first step is to **harvest** the oranges.

7

Then, the oranges are put into a big truck called a **goat**.

9

After that, the goat is driven to the juice **factory**.

11

Next, the oranges are cleaned.

Then, a worker **inspects** the oranges.

She makes sure all the fruit is good to eat.

After that, it's time to
make juice!

The oranges are placed in a
machine that squeezes the fruit.

Juice pours out.

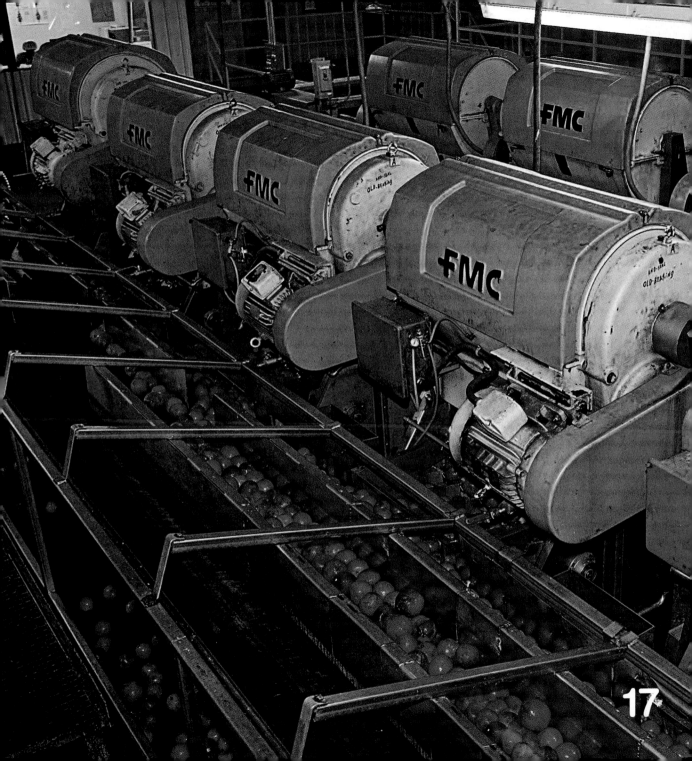

17

The juice is poured into bottles. Then, a machine puts caps on the bottles. The bottles are ready to be sent to stores.

19

Finally, the juice is ready to drink!

Orange juice is healthy
and **delicious.**

Words to Know

delicious (dee-LI-shus) – tasty

factory (FAK-tuh-ree) – a building that is filled with machines that make many things

goat (GOTE) – a large truck, or fruit loader, used for collecting oranges

harvest (HAR-vest) – to collect fruits or vegetables from the fields

inspects (in-SPEKTZ) – checks for problems

machine (muh-SHEEN) – equipment with moving parts that are used to do a job

Find Out More

Books

From Oranges to Orange Juice

Kristin Thoennes Keller

Capstone Press

Orange Juice Before the Store

Ryan Jacobson

Child's World Incorporated

Website

How Do They Do It?

science.discovery.com/tv-shows/how-do-they-do-it/videos/how-do-they-do-it-how-is-orange-juice-made.htm

Index